Animism, Magic and the Omnipotence of Thought

By Sigmund Freud

Copyright © 2021 Lamp of Trismegistus. All rights reserved. No part of this publication may be reproduced or transmitted in any form or by any means, electronic or mechanical, including photocopying, recording, or by any information storage and retrieval system, without permission in writing from Lamp of Trismegistus. Reviewers may quote brief passages.

ISBN: 978-1-63118-568-7

Esoteric Classics

Other Books in this Series and Related Titles

Aurora of the Philosophers by Paracelsus (978-1-63118-507-6)

Clairvoyance and Psychic Abilities by A Besant &c (978-1-63118-403-1)

The Feminine Occult by various authors (978-1-63118-711-7)

Rosicrucian Rules, Secret Signs, Codes and Symbols by various (978-1-63118-488-8)

An Outline of Theosophy by C W Leadbeater (978-1-63118-452-9)

Paracelsus, the Four Elements and Their Spirits by M P Hall (978-1-63118-400-0)

Essays on Ancient Magic by Helena P Blavatsky (978-1-63118-535-9)

Essays on the Esoteric Tradition of Karma by A Besant &c (978-1-63118-426-0)

The Use of Evil by Annie Besant (978-1-63118-532-8)

The Alchemical Catechism of Paracelsus by Paracelsus (978-1-63118-513-7)

Alchemy in the Nineteenth Century by Helena P Blavatsky (978-1-63118-446-8)

Qabbalistic Teachings and the Tree of Life by M P Hall (978-1-63118-482-6)

The Historic, Mythic and Mystic Christ by Annie Besant (978–1–63118–533–5)

The Hidden Mysteries of Christianity by Annie Besant (978–1–63118–534–2)

History, Analysis and Secret Tradition of the Tarot by Hall &c (978-1-63118-445-1)

Crystal Vision Through Crystal Gazing by Frater Achad (978-1-63118-455-0)

The Golden Verses of Pythagoras: Five Translations (978-1-63118-479-6)

Arcane Formulas or Mental Alchemy by W W Atkinson (978-1-63118-459-8)

The Machinery of the Mind by Dion Fortune (978-1-63118-451-2)

The A E Waite Reader: A Selection of Occult Essays (978-1-63118-515-1)

The Leadbeater Reader: A Selection of Occult Essays (978-1-63118-483-3)

Audio versions are also available on Audible, Amazon and Apple

Other Books in this Series and Related Titles

Buddhism by F Otto Schrader (978–1–63118–567–0)

Death by W W Westcott (978–1–63118–566–3)

The Religion of Theosophy by Bhagwan Das (978–1–63118–565–6)

The Spirit of Zoroastrianism by Henry S Olcott (978–1–63118–564–9)

The Brotherhood of Religions by Annie Besant (978–1–63118–563–2)

Fourth Book of Maccabees by Josephus (978-1-63118-562-5)

The Story of Ahikar by Ahiqar (978-1-63118-561-8)

Vision of the Spirit by C. Jinarajadasa (978-1-63118-560-1)

Occult Arts by William Q. Judge (978-1-63118-559-5)

Kali the Mother by Sister Nivedita (978-1-63118-558-8)

Love and Death by Sri Aurobindo (978–1–63118–557–1)

Times and Seasons Volume 1, Numbers 4-6 (978-1-63118-556-4)

The Book of John Whitmer by John Whitmer (978-1-63118-554-0)

Interesting Account of Several Remarkable Visions (978-1-63118-553-3)

The Evening and Morning Star Volume 1, Numbers 11 & 12 (978-1-63118-552-6)

Private Diary of Joseph Smith 1832-1834 (978-1-63118-546-5)

An Address to All Believers in Christ Elder David Whitmer (978-1-63118-545-8)

A Manuscript on Far West by Reed Peck (978-1-63118-544-1)

The Story of Mormonism by James E Talmage (978-1-63118-543-4)

The Philosophy of Mormonism by James E Talmage (978-1-63118-542-7)

The Angel of the Prairies or A Dream of the Future (978-1-63118-541-0)

Audio versions are also available on Audible, Amazon and Apple

Table of Contents

Introduction…7

Animism, Magic and the Omnipotence of Thought

PART I…9

PART II…13

PART III…23

PART IV…29

INTRODUCTION

The word "esoteric" can be difficult to define. Esotericism in general can be seen less as a system of beliefs and more as a category, which encompasses numerous, different systems of beliefs. It's a bit of juxtaposition, since the word "esoteric" indicates something that few people know about, while the term itself broadly covers numerous philosophies, practices, areas of study and belief systems.

In a greater sense, Esotericism acts as a storehouse for secret knowledge, which is often considered ancient (by *tradition, if not by fact*), passed down from generation to generation, in private. At various times in history, simply possessing the knowledge of some of these subjects, was considered illegal and a jailable offence, if discovered. This usually included such general topics as Alchemy, Pharmacology, Qabalah, Hermeticism, Occultism, Ceremonial Magic, Astrology, Divination, Rosicrucianism and so on. Collectively, these areas of study were often referred to as the esoteric sciences.

Sometimes, the outer garment of a subject isn't esoteric, while what is hidden beneath it, is. As an example, Freemasonry isn't necessarily esoteric by nature (at *least not anymore*), but certain signs, passwords and handshakes given to the candidate during their initiation, are in fact, esoteric, in the sense that they are hidden from the general public.

Today, in the twenty-first century, such topics are readily available at bookstores across the country, and numerous mainsteam publishers offer beginners guides and coffee-table volumes on many of these subjects, intended for mass appeal. Books like *"The Secret"* have turned previously arcane topics into household knowledge. All that being the case, however, it isn't to say that there still aren't buried secrets to uncover, ancient wisdom being ignored and forgotten mysteries to be explored. In fact, it is often that we are only able to further our own studies by standing on the shoulders of these disappearing giants.

Lamp of Trismegistus is doing its part to help preserve humanity's esoteric history by making some of these classics available to those students who are seeking to unearth the knowledge of these ancient colossi.

So, be sure to check other titles from our *Esoteric Classics* series, as well as our *Occult Fiction, Theosophical Classics, Foundations of Freemasonry Series, Supernatural Fiction, Paranormal Research Series, Studies in Buddhism* and our *Christian Apocrypha Series.* You can also download the audio versions of most of these titles from Amazon, Apple or Audible, for learning on the go.

ANIMISM, MAGIC AND THE OMNIPOTENCE OF THOUGHT

PART I

It is a necessary defect of studies which seek to apply the point of view of psychoanalysis to the mental sciences that they cannot do justice to either subject. They therefore confine themselves to the role of incentives and make suggestions to the expert which he should take into consideration in his work. This defect will make itself felt most strongly in an essay such as this which tries to treat of the enormous sphere called animism.[1]

Animism in the narrower sense is the theory of psychic concepts and in the wider sense, of spiritual beings in general. Animatism, the animation theory of seemingly inanimate nature, is a further subdivision which also includes animatism and animism. The name animism, formerly applied to a definite philosophic system, seems to have acquired its present meaning through E. B. Tylor.[2]

What led to the formulation of these names is the insight into the very remarkable conceptions of nature and the world of those primitive races known to us from history and from our own times. These races populate the world with a multitude of spiritual beings

---

[1] The necessary crowding of the material also compels us to dispense with a thorough bibliography. Instead of this the reader is referred to the well-known works of Herbert Spencer, J. G. Frazer, A. Lang, E. B. Tylor and W. Wundt, from which all the statements concerning animism and magic are taken. The independence of the author can manifest itself only in the choice of the material and of opinions.

[2] E. B. Tylor, "Primitive Culture," Vol. I, p. 425, fourth ed., 1903. W. Wundt, "Myth and Religion," Vol. II, p. 173, 1906.

which are benevolent or malevolent to them, and attribute the causation of natural processes to these spirits and demons; they also consider that not only animals and plants, but inanimate things as well are animated by them. A third and perhaps the most important part of this primitive "nature philosophy" seems far less striking to us because we ourselves are not yet far enough removed from it, though we have greatly limited the existence of spirits and to-day explain the processes of nature by the assumption of impersonal physical forces. For primitive people believe in a similar "animation" of human individuals as well. Human beings have souls which can leave their habitation and enter into other beings; these souls are the bearers of spiritual activities and are, to a certain extent, independent of the "bodies." Originally souls were thought of as being very similar to individuals; only in the course of a long evolution did they lose their material character and attain a high degree of "spiritualization."[3]

Most authors incline to the assumption that these soul conceptions are the original nucleus of the animistic system, that spirits merely correspond to souls that have become independent, and that the souls of animals, plants and things were formed after the analogy of human souls.

How did primitive people come to the peculiarly dualistic fundamental conceptions on which this animistic system rests? Through the observation, it is thought, of the phenomena of sleep (with dreams) and death which resemble sleep, and through the effort to explain these conditions, which affect each individual so intimately. Above all, the problem of death must have become the starting point of the formation of the theory. To primitive man the continuation of life—immortality—would be self-evident. The

---

[3] Wundt 1. c., Chapter IV, "Die Seelenvorstellungen."

conception of death is something accepted later, and only with hesitation, for even to us it is still devoid of content and unrealizable. Very likely discussions have taken place over the part which may have been played by other observations and experiences in the formation of the fundamental animistic conceptions such as dream imagery, shadows and reflections, but these have led to no conclusion.[4]

If primitive man reacted to the phenomena that stimulated his reflection with the formation of conceptions of the soul, and then transferred these to objects of the outer world, his attitude will be judged to be quite natural and in no way mysterious. In view of the fact that animistic conceptions have been shown to be similar among the most varied races and in all periods, Wundt states that these "are the necessary psychological product of the myth forming consciousness, and primitive animism may be looked upon as the spiritual expression of man's natural state in so far as this is at all accessible to our observation."[5] Hume has already justified the animation of the inanimate in his "Natural History of Religions," where he said: "There is a universal tendency among mankind to conceive all beings like themselves and to transfer to every object those qualities with which they are familiarly acquainted and of which they are intimately conscious."[6]

Animism is a system of thought, it gives not only the explanation of a single phenomenon, but makes it possible to comprehend the totality of the world from one point, as a continuity. Writers maintain that in the course of time three such

---

[4] Compare, besides Wundt and H. Spencer and the instructive article in the "Encyclopedia Britannica," 1911 (Animism, Mythology, and so forth).

[5] l. c., p. 154.

[6] See Tylor, "Primitive Culture," Vol. I, p. 477.

systems of thought, three great world systems came into being: the animistic (mythological), the religious, and the scientific. Of these animism, the first system is perhaps the most consistent and the most exhaustive, and the one which explains the nature of the world in its entirety. This first world system of mankind is now a psychological theory. It would go beyond our scope to show how much of it can still be demonstrated in the life of to-day, either as a worthless survival in the form of superstition, or in living form, as the foundation of our language, our belief, and our philosophy.

It is in reference to the successive stages of these three world systems that we say that animism in itself was not yet a religion but contained the prerequisites from which religions were later formed. It is also evident that myths are based upon animistic foundations, but the detailed relation of myths to animism seem unexplained in some essential points.

PART II

Our psychoanalytic work will begin at a different point. It must not be assumed that mankind came to create its first world system through a purely speculative thirst for knowledge. The practical need of mastering the world must have contributed to this effort. We are therefore not astonished to learn that something else went hand in hand with the animistic system, namely the elaboration of directions for making oneself master of men, animals and things, as well as of their spirits. S. Reinach[7] wants to call these directions, which are known under the names of "sorcery and magic," the strategy of animism; With Mauss and Hubert, I should prefer to compare them to a technique.[8]

Can the conceptions of sorcery and magic be separated? It can be done if we are willing on our own authority to put ourselves above the vagaries of linguistic usage. Then sorcery is essentially the art of influencing spirits by treating them like people under the same circumstances, that is to say by appeasing them, reconciling them, making them more favorably disposed to one, by intimidating them, by depriving them of their power and by making them subject to one's will; all that is accomplished through the same methods that have been found effective with living people. Magic, however, is something else; it does not essentially concern itself with spirits, and uses special means, not the ordinary psychological method. We can easily guess that magic is the earlier and the more important part of animistic technique, for among the means with which spirits are to

---

[7] "Cultes, Mythes et Religions," T. II, Introduction, p. XV, 1909.
[8] "Année Sociologique," Seventh Vol., 1904.

be treated there are also found the magic kind,⁹ and magic is also applied where spiritualization of nature has not yet, as it seems to us, been accomplished.

Magic must serve the most varied purposes. It must subject the processes of nature to the will of man, protect the individual against enemies and dangers, and give him the power to injure his enemies. But the principles on whose assumptions the magic activity is based, or rather the principle of magic, is so evident that it was recognized by all authors. If we may take the opinion of E. B. Tylor at its face value it can be most tersely expressed in his words: "mistaking an ideal connection for a real one." We shall explain this characteristic in the case of two groups of magic acts.

One of the most widespread magic procedures for injuring an enemy consists of making an effigy of him out of any kind of material. The likeness counts for little, in fact any object may be "named" as his image. Whatever is subsequently done to this image will also happen to the hated prototype; thus if the effigy has been injured in any place he will be afflicted by a disease in the corresponding part of the body. This same magic technique, instead of being used for private enmity can also be employed for pious purposes and can thus be used to aid the gods against evil demons. I quote Frazer:[10] "Every night when the sun-god Ra in ancient Egypt sank to his home in the glowing west he was assailed by hosts of demons under the leadership of the archfiend Apepi. All night long he fought them, and sometimes by day the powers of darkness sent up clouds even into the blue Egyptian sky to obscure his light and weaken his power. To aid the sun-god in this daily struggle, a

---

[9] To frighten away a ghost with noise and cries is a form of pure sorcery; to force him to do something by taking his name is to employ magic against him.
[10] "The Magic Art," II, p. 67.

ceremony was daily performed in his temple at Thebes. A figure of his foe Apepi, represented as a crocodile with a hideous face or a serpent with many coils, was made of wax, and on it the demon's name was written in green ink. Wrapt in a papyrus case, on which another likeness of Apepi had been drawn in green ink, the figure was then tied up with black hair, spat upon, hacked with a stone knife and cast on the ground. There the priest trod on it with his left foot again and again, and then burned it in a fire made of a certain plant or grass. When Apepi himself had thus been effectively disposed of, waxen effigies of each of his principal demons, and of their fathers, mothers, and children, were made and burnt in the same way. The service, accompanied by the recitation of certain prescribed spells, was repeated not merely morning, noon and night, but whenever a storm was raging or heavy rain had set in, or black clouds were stealing across the sky to hide the sun's bright disk. The fiends of darkness, clouds and rain, felt the injury inflicted on their images as if it had been done to themselves; they passed away, at least for a time, and the beneficent sun-god shone out triumphant once more."[11]

There is a great mass of magic actions which show a similar motivation but I shall lay stress upon only two, which have always played a great role among primitive races and which have been partly preserved in the myths and cults of higher stages of evolution: the art of causing rain and fruitfulness by magic. Rain is produced by magic means, by imitating it, and perhaps also by imitating the clouds and storm which produce it. It looks as if they wanted to "play rain." The Ainos of Japan, for instance, make rain by pouring out water through a big sieve, while others fit out a big bowl with

---

[11] The Biblical prohibition against making an image of anything living hardly sprang from any fundamental rejection of plastic art, but was probably meant to deprive magic, which the Hebraic religion proscribed, of one of its instruments. Frazer, 1. c., p. 87, note.

sails and oars as if it were a ship, which is then dragged about the village and gardens. But the fruitfulness of the soil was assured by magic means by showing it the spectacle of human sexual intercourse. To cite one out of many examples; in some part of Java, the peasants used to go out into the fields at night for sexual intercourse when the rice was about to blossom in order to stimulate the rice to fruitfulness through their example.[12] At the same time it was feared that proscribed incestuous relationships would stimulate the soil to grow weeds and render it unfruitful.[13]

Certain negative rules, that is to say magic precautions, must be put into this first group. If some of the inhabitants of a Dayak village had set out on a hunt for wild-boars, those remaining behind were in the meantime not permitted to touch either oil or water with their hands, as such acts would soften the hunters' fingers and would let the quarry slip through their hands.[14] Or when a Gilyak hunter was pursuing game in the woods, his children were forbidden to make drawings on wood or in the sand, as the paths in the thick woods might become as intertwined as the lines of the drawing, and the hunter would not find his way home.[15]

The fact that in these as in a great many other examples of magic influence, distance plays no part, telepathy is taken as a matter of course—will cause us no difficulties in grasping the peculiarity of magic.

There is no doubt about what is considered the effective force in all these examples. It is the *similarity* between the performed

---

[12] "The Magic Art," II, p. 98.
[13] An echo of this is to be found in the "Oedipus Rex" of Sophocles.
[14] "The Magic Art," p. 120.
[15] 1. c., p. 122.

action and the expected happening. Frazer therefore calls this kind of magic *imitative* or *homeopathic*. If I want it to rain I only have to produce something that looks like rain or recalls rain. In a later phase of cultural development, instead of these magic conjurations of rain, processions are arranged to a house of god, in order to supplicate the saint who dwells there to send rain. Finally also this religious technique will be given up and instead an effort will be made to find out what would influence the atmosphere to produce rain.

In another group of magic actions the principle of similarity is no longer involved, but in its stead there is another principle the nature of which is well brought out in the following examples.

Another method may be used to injure an enemy. You possess yourself of his hair, his nails, anything that he has discarded, or even a part of his clothing, and do something hostile to these things. This is just as effective as if you had dominated the person himself, and anything that you do to the things that belong to him must happen to him too. According to the conception of primitive men a name is an essential part of a personality; if therefore you know the name of a person or a spirit you have acquired a certain power over its bearer. This explains the remarkable precautions and restrictions in the use of names which we have touched upon in the essay on taboo.[16] In these examples similarity is evidently replaced by relationship.

The cannibalism of primitive races derives its more sublime motivation in a similar manner. By absorbing parts of the body of a person through the act of eating we also come to possess the properties which belonged to that person. From this there follow precautions and restrictions as to diet under special circumstances.

---

[16] See preceding chapter, p. 92.

Thus a pregnant woman will avoid eating the meat of certain animals because their undesirable properties, for example, cowardice, might thus be transferred to the child she is nourishing. It makes no difference to the magic influence whether the connection is already abolished or whether it had consisted of only one very important contact. Thus, for instance, the belief in a magic bond which links the fate of a wound with the weapon which caused it can be followed unchanged through thousands of years. If a Melanesian gets possession of the bow by which he was wounded he will carefully keep it in a cool place in order thus to keep down the inflammation of the wound. But if the bow has remained in the possession of the enemy it will certainly be kept in close proximity to a fire in order that the wound may burn and become thoroughly inflamed. Pliny, in his Natural History XXVIII, advises spitting on the hand which has caused the injury if one regrets having injured some one; the pain of the injured person will then immediately be eased. Francis Bacon, in his Natural History, mentions the generally accredited belief that putting a salve on the weapon which has made a wound will cause this wound to heal of itself. It is said that even today English peasants follow this prescription, and that if they have cut themselves with a scythe they will from that moment on carefully keep the instrument clean in order that the wound may not fester. In June, 1902, a local English weekly reported that a woman called Matilde Henry of Norwich accidentally ran an iron nail into the sole of her foot. Without having the wound examined or even taking off her stocking she bade her daughter to oil the nail thoroughly, in the expectation that then nothing could happen to her. She died a few days later of tetanus[17] in consequence of postponed antisepsis.

The examples from this last group illustrate Frazer's distinction between *contagious* magic and *imitative* magic. What is considered as

---

[17] Frazer, "The Magic Art," p. 201-203

effective in these examples is no longer the similarity, but the association in space, the contiguity, or at least the imagined contiguity, or the memory of its existence. But since similarity and contiguity are the two essential principles of the processes of association of ideas, it must be concluded that the dominance of associations of ideas really explains all the madness of the rules of magic. We can see how true Tylor's quoted characteristic of magic: "mistaking an ideal connection for a real one," proves to be. The same may be said of Frazer's idea, who has expressed it in almost the same terms: "men mistook the order of their ideas for the order of nature, and hence imagined that the control which they have, or seem to have, over their thoughts, permitted them to have a corresponding control over things."[18]

It will at first seem strange that this illuminating explanation of magic could have been rejected by some authors as unsatisfactory.[19] But on closer consideration we must sustain the objection that the association theory of magic merely explains the paths that magic travels, and not its essential nature, that is, it does not explain the misunderstanding which bids it put psychological laws in place of natural ones. We are apparently in need here of a dynamic factor; but while the search for this leads the critics of Frazer's theory astray, it will be easy to give a satisfactory explanation of magic by carrying its association theory further and by entering more deeply into it.

First let us examine the simpler and more important case of imitative magic. According to Frazer this may be practiced by itself, whereas contagious magic as a rule presupposes the imitative.[20] The motives which impel one to exercise magic are easily recognized;

---

[18] "The Magic Art," p. 420.

[19] Compare the article "Magic" (N. T. W.) Encyclopedia Britannica, 11th Ed.

[20] l. c., p. 54.

they are the wishes of men. We need only assume that primitive man had great confidence in the power of his wishes. At bottom everything which he accomplished by magic means must have been done solely because he wanted it. Thus in the beginning only his wish is accentuated.

In the case of the child which finds itself under analogous psychic conditions, without being as yet capable of motor activity, we have elsewhere advocated the assumption that it at first really satisfies its wishes by means of hallucinations, in that it creates the satisfying situation through centrifugal excitements of its sensory organs.[21] The adult primitive man knows another way. A motor impulse, the will, clings to his wish and this will which later will change the face of the earth in the service of wish fulfillment is now used to represent the gratification so that one may experience it, as it were, through motor hallucination. Such a *representation* of the gratified wish is altogether comparable to the *play* of children, where it replaces the purely sensory technique of gratification. If play and imitative representation suffice for the child and for primitive man, it must not be taken as a sign of modesty, in our sense, or of resignation due to the realization of their impotence, on the contrary, it is the very obvious result of the excessive valuation of their wish, of the will which depends upon the wish and of the paths the wish takes. In time the psychic accent is displaced from the motives of the magic act to its means, namely to the act itself. Perhaps it would be more correct to say that primitive man does not become aware of the over-valuation of his psychic acts until it becomes evident to him through the means employed. It would also seem as if it were the magic act itself which compels the fulfillment of the wish by virtue of its similarity to the object desired. At the

---

[21] Formulation of two principles of psychic activity, "Jahrb. für Psychoanalyt. Forschungen," Vol. III, 1912, p. 2

stage of animistic thinking there is as yet no way of demonstrating objectively the true state of affairs, but this becomes possible at later stages when, though such procedures are still practiced, the psychic phenomenon of skepticism already manifests itself as a tendency to repression. At that stage men will acknowledge that the conjuration of spirits avails nothing unless accompanied by belief, and that the magic effect of prayer fails if there is no piety behind it.[22]

The possibility of a contagious magic which depends upon contiguous association will then show us that the psychic valuation of the wish and the will has been extended to all psychic acts which the will can command. We may say that at present there is a general over-valuation of all psychic processes, that is to say there is an attitude towards the world which according to our understanding of the relation of reality to thought must appear like an over-estimation of the latter. Objects as such are over-shadowed by the ideas representing them; what takes place in the latter must also happen to the former and the relations which exist between ideas are also postulated as to things. As thought does not recognize distances and easily brings together in one act of consciousness things spatially and temporally far removed, the magic world also puts itself above spatial distance by telepathy, and treats a past association as if it were a present one. In the animistic age the reflection of the inner world must obscure that other picture of the world which we believe we recognize.

Let us also point out that the two principles of association, similarity and contiguity, meet in the higher unity of contact. Association by contiguity is contact in the direct sense, and

---

[22] The King in "Hamlet" (Act III, Scene 4):

"My words fly up, my thoughts remain below,
Words without thoughts never to heaven go."

association by similarity is contact in the transferred sense. Another identity in the psychic process which has not yet been grasped by us is probably concealed in the use of the same word for both kinds of associations. It is the same range of the concept of contact which we have found in the analysis of taboo.[23]

In summing up we may now say that the principle which controls magic, and the technique of the animistic method of thought, is "Omnipotence of Thought."

---

[23] Compare with *Taboo and the Ambivalence of Emotions*.

PART III

I have adopted the term "Omnipotence of Thought" from a highly intelligent man, a former sufferer from compulsion neurosis, who, after being cured through psychoanalytic treatment, was able to demonstrate his efficiency and good sense.[24] He had coined this phrase to designate all those peculiar and uncanny occurrences which seemed to pursue him just as they pursue others afflicted with his malady. Thus if he happened to think of a person, he was actually confronted with this person as if he had conjured him up; if he inquired suddenly about the state of health of an acquaintance whom he had long missed he was sure to hear that this acquaintance had just died, so that he could believe that the deceased had drawn his attention to himself by telepathic means; if he uttered a half meant imprecation against a stranger, he could expect to have him die soon thereafter and burden him with the responsibility for his death. He was able to explain most of these cases in the course of the treatment, he could tell how the illusion had originated, and what he himself had contributed towards furthering his superstitious expectations.[25] All compulsion neurotics are superstitious in this manner and often against their better judgment.

The existence of omnipotence of thought is most clearly seen in compulsion neurosis, where the results of this primitive method of thought are most often found or met in consciousness. But we must guard against seeing in this a distinguishing characteristic of this neurosis, for analytic investigation reveals the same mechanism

---

[24] Remarks upon a case of Compulsion Neurosis, "Jahrb. für Psychoanalyt. und Psychopath. Forschungen," Vol. I, 1909.
[25] We seem to attribute the character of the "uncanny" to all such impressions which seek to confirm the omnipotence of thought and the animistic method of thought in general, though our judgment has long rejected it.

in the other neuroses. In every one of the neuroses it is not the reality of the experience but the reality of the thought which forms the basis for the symptom formation. Neurotics live in a special world in which, as I have elsewhere expressed it, only the "neurotic standard of currency" counts, that is to say, only things intensively thought of or affectively conceived are effective with them, regardless of whether these things are in harmony with outer reality. The hysteric repeats in his attacks and fixates through his symptoms, occurrences which have taken place only in his phantasy, though in the last analysis they go back to real events or have been built up from them. The neurotic's guilty conscience is just as incomprehensible if traced to real misdeeds. A compulsion neurotic may be oppressed by a sense of guilt which is appropriate to a wholesale murderer, while at the same time he acts towards his fellow beings in a most considerate and scrupulous manner, a behavior which he evinced since his childhood. And yet his sense of guilt is justified; it is based upon intensive and frequent death wishes which unconsciously manifest themselves towards his fellow beings. It is motivated from the point of view of unconscious thoughts, but not of intentional acts. Thus the omnipotence of thought, the overestimation of psychic processes as opposed to reality, proves to be of unlimited effect in the neurotic's affective life and in all that emanates from it. But if we subject him to psychoanalytic treatment, which makes his unconscious thoughts conscious to him, he refuses to believe that thoughts are free and is always afraid to express evil wishes lest they be fulfilled in consequence of his utterance. But through this attitude as well as through the superstition which plays an active part in his life he reveals to us how close he stands to the savage who believes he can change the outer world by a mere thought of his.

The primary obsessive actions of these neurotics are really altogether of a magical nature. If not magic they are at least anti-magic and are destined to ward off the expectation of evil with which the neurosis is wont to begin. Whenever I was able to pierce these secrets it turned out that the content of this expectation of evil was death. According to Schopenhauer the problem of death stands at the beginning of every philosophy; we have heard that the formation of the soul conception and of the belief in demons which characterize animism, are also traced back to the impression which death makes upon man. It is hard to decide whether these first compulsive and protective actions follow the principle of similarity, or of contrast, for under the conditions of the neurosis they are usually distorted through displacement upon some trifle, upon some action which in itself is quite insignificant.[26] The protective formulas of the compulsion neurosis also have a counterpart in the incantations of magic. But the evolution of compulsive actions may be described by pointing out how these actions begin as a spell against evil wishes which are very remote from anything sexual, only to end up as a substitute for forbidden sexual activity, which they imitate as faithfully as possible.

If we accept the evolution of man's conceptions of the universe mentioned above, according to which the *animistic* phase is *succeeded* by the *religious*, and this in turn by the *scientific*, we have no difficulty in following the fortunes of the "omnipotence of thought" through all these phases. In the animistic stage man ascribes omnipotence to himself; in the religious he has ceded it to the gods, but without seriously giving it up, for he reserves to himself the right to control the gods by influencing them in some way or other in the interest of his wishes. In the scientific attitude towards life there is no longer any room for man's omnipotence; he has acknowledged his smallness and has submitted to death as to all other natural

---

[26] The following discussions will yield a further motive for this displacement upon a trivial action.

necessities in a spirit of resignation. Nevertheless, in our reliance upon the power of the human spirit which copes with the laws of reality, there still lives on a fragment of this primitive belief in the omnipotence of thought.

In retracing the development of libidinous impulses in the individual from its mature form back to its first beginnings in childhood, we at first found an important distinction which is stated in the "Three Contributions to the Theory of Sex."[27] The manifestations of sexual impulses can be recognized from the beginning but at first they are not yet directed to any outer object. Each individual component of the sexual impulse works for a gain in pleasure and finds its gratification in its own body. This stage is called *autoerotism* and is distinguished from the stage of object selection.

In the course of further study it proved to be practical and really necessary to insert a third stage between these two or, if one prefers, to divide the first stage of autoerotism into two. In this intermediary stage, the importance of which increases the more we investigate it, the sexual impulses which formerly were separate, have already formed into a unit and have also found an object; but this object is not external and foreign to the individual, but is his own ego, which is formed at this period. This new stage is called *narcism*, in view of the pathological fixation of this condition which may be observed later on. The individual acts as if he were in love with himself; for the purposes of our analysis the ego impulses and the libidinous wishes cannot yet be separated from each other.

Although this narcistic stage, in which the hitherto dissociated sexual impulses combine into a unity and take the ego as their object,

---

[27] Monograph Series, 1916.

cannot as yet be sharply differentiated, we can already surmise that the narcistic organization is never altogether given up again. To a certain extent man remains narcistic, even after he has found outer objects for his libido, and the objects upon which he bestows it represent, as it were, emanations of the libido which remain with his ego and which can be withdrawn into it. The state of being in love, so remarkable psychologically, and the normal prototype of the psychoses, corresponds to the highest stage of these emanations, in contrast to the state of self-love.

This high estimation of psychic acts found among primitives and neurotics, which we feel to be an overestimation, may now appropriately be brought into relation to narcism, and interpreted as an essential part of it. We would say that among primitive people thinking is still highly sexualized and that this accounts for the belief in the omnipotence of thought, the unshaken confidence in the capacity to dominate the world and the inaccessibility to the obvious facts which could enlighten man as to his real place in the world. In the case of neurotics a considerable part of this primitive attitude has remained as a constitutional factor, while on the other hand the sexual repression occurring in them has brought about a new sexualization of the processes of thought. In both cases, whether we deal with an original libidinous investment of thought or whether the same process has been accomplished regressively, the psychic results are the same, namely, intellectual narcism and omnipotence of thought.[28] If we may take the now established omnipotence of thought among primitive races as a proof of their narcism, we may venture to compare the various evolutionary stages of man's conception of the universe with the stages of the libidinous

---

[28] It is almost an axiom with writers on this subject, that a sort of "Solipsism or Berkleianism" (as Professor Sully terms it as as he finds it in the child) operates in the savage to make him refuse to recognize death as a fact.—Marett, "Pre-animistic Religion, Folklore," Vol. XI, 1900, p. 178.

evolution of the individual. We find that the animistic phase corresponds in time as well as in content with narcism, the religious phase corresponds to that stage of object finding which is characterized by dependence on the parents, while the scientific stage has its full counterpart in the individual's state of maturity where, having renounced the pleasure principle and having adapted himself to reality, he seeks his object in the outer world.[29]

Only in one field has the omnipotence of thought been retained in our own civilization, namely in art. In art alone it still happens that man, consumed by his wishes, produces something similar to the gratification of these wishes and this playing, thanks to artistic illusion, calls forth affects as if it were something real. We rightly speak of the magic of art and compare the artist with a magician. But this comparison is perhaps more important than it claims to be. Art, which certainly did not begin as art for art's sake, originally served tendencies which to-day have for the greater part ceased to exist. Among these we may suspect various magic intentions.[30]

---

[29] We merely wish to indicate here that the original narcism of the child is decisive for the interpretation of its character development and that it precludes the assumption of a primitive feeling of inferiority for the child.

[30] S. Reinach, "L'art et la Magie," in the collection, "Cultes, Mythes et Religions," Vol. I, p. 125-136. Reinach thinks that the primitive artists who have left us the scratched or painted animal pictures in the caves of France did not want to "arouse" pleasure, but to "conjure things." He explains this by showing that these drawings are in the darkest and most inaccessible part of the caves and that representations of feared beasts of prey are absent. "Les modernes parlent souvent, par hyperbole, de la magie du pinceau ou du ciseau d'un grand artiste et, en général, de la magie de l'art. Entendu en sense propre, qui est celui d'une constrainte mystique exercée par la volonté de l'homme sur d'autres volontés ou sur les choses, cette expression n'est plus admissible; mais nous avons vu qu'elle était autrefois rigouresement vraie, du moins dans l'opinion des artistes" (p. 136).

PART IV

Animism, the first conception of the world which man succeeded in evolving, was therefore psychological. It did not yet require any science to establish it, for science sets in only after we have realized that we do not know the world and that we must therefore seek means of getting to know it. But animism was natural and self-evident to primitive man; he knew how the things of the world were constituted, and as man conceived himself to be. We are therefore prepared to find that primitive man transferred the structural relations of his own psyche to the outer world,[31] and on the other hand we may make the attempt to transfer back into the human soul what animism teaches about the nature of things.

Magic, the technique of animism, clearly and unmistakably shows the tendency of forcing the laws of psychic life upon the reality of things, under conditions where spirits did not yet have to play any role, and could still be taken as objects of magic treatment. The assumptions of magic are therefore of older origin than the spirit theory, which forms the nucleus of animism. Our psychoanalytic view here coincides with a theory of R. R. Marett, according to which animism is preceded by a pre-animistic stage the nature of which is best indicated by the name Animatism (the theory of general animation). We have practically no further knowledge of pre-animism, as no race has yet been found without conceptions of spirits.[32]

---

[31] Recognized through so-called endopsychic perceptions.
[32] R. R. Marett, "Pre-animistic Religion, Folklore," Vol. XI, No. 2, London, 1900.—Comp. Wundt, "Myth and Religion," Vol. II, p. 171.

While magic still retains the full omnipotence of ideas, animism has ceded part of this omnipotence to spirits and thus has started on the way to form a religion. Now what could have moved primitive man to this first act of renunciation? It could hardly have been an insight into the incorrectness of his assumptions, for he continued to retain the magic technique.

As pointed out elsewhere, spirits and demons were nothing but the projection of primitive man's emotional impulses;[33] he personified the things he endowed with affects, populated the world with them and then rediscovered his inner psychic processes outside himself, quite like the ingenious paranoiac Schreber, who found the fixations and detachments of his libido reflected in the fates of the "God-rays" which he invented.[34]

As on a former occasion,[35] we want to avoid the problem as to the origin of the tendency to project psychic processes into the outer world. It is fair to assume, however, that this tendency becomes stronger where the projection into the outer world offers psychic relief. Such a state of affairs can with certainty be expected if the impulses struggling for omnipotence have come into conflict with each other, for then they evidently cannot all become omnipotent. The morbid process in paranoia actually uses the mechanism of projection to solve such conflicts which arise in the psychic life. However, it so happens that the model case of such a conflict between two parts of an antithesis is the ambivalent attitude which we have analyzed in detail in the situation of the mourner at the death of one dear to him. Such a case appeals to us as especially

---

[33] We assume that in this early narcistic stage feelings from libidinous and other sources of excitement are perhaps still indistinguishably combined with each other.

[34] Schreber, "Denwürdigkeiten eines Nervenkranken," 1903.—Freud, Psychoanalytic Observations concerning an autobiographically described case of Paranoia, "Jahrbuch für Psychoanalyt. Forsch," Vol. III, 1911.

[35] Compare the latest communication about the Schreber case, p. 59.

fitted to motivate the creation of projection formations. Here again we are in agreement with those authors who declare that evil spirits were the first born among spirits, and who find the origin of soul conceptions in the impression which death makes upon the survivors. We differ from them only in not putting the intellectual problem which death imposes upon the living into the foreground, instead of which we transfer the force which stimulates inquiry to the conflict of feelings into which this situation plunges the survivor.

The first theoretical accomplishment of man, the creation of spirits, would therefore spring from the same source as the first moral restrictions to which he subjects himself, namely, the rules of taboo. But the fact that they have the same source should not prejudice us in favor of a simultaneous origin. If it really were the situation of the survivor confronted by the dead which first caused primitive man to reflect, so that he was compelled to surrender some of his omnipotence to spirits and to sacrifice a part of the free will of his actions, these cultural creations would be a first recognition of the ἀνάγκη, which opposes man's narcism. Primitive man would bow to the superior power of death with the same gesture with which he seems to deny it.

If we have the courage to follow our assumptions further, we may ask what essential part of our psychological structure is reflected and reviewed in the projection formation of souls and spirits. It is then difficult to dispute that the primitive conception of the soul, though still far removed from the later and wholly immaterial soul, nevertheless shares its nature and therefore looks upon a person or thing as a duality, over the two elements of which the known properties and changes of the whole are distributed. This origin duality, we have borrowed the term from Herbert

Spencer,[36] is already identical with the dualism which manifests itself in our customary separation of spirit from body, and whose indestructible linguistic manifestations we recognize, for instance, in the description of a person who faints or raves as one who is "beside himself."[37]

The thing which we, just like primitive man, project into outer reality, can hardly be anything else than the recognition of a state in which a given thing is present to the senses and to consciousness, next to which another state exists in which the thing is *latent*, but can reappear, that is to say, the co-existence of perception and memory, or, to generalize it, the existence of unconscious psychic processes next to conscious ones.[38] It might be said that in the last analysis the "spirit" of a person or a thing is the faculty of remembering and representing the object, after he or it was withdrawn from conscious perception.

Of course we must not expect from either the primitive or the current conception of the "soul" that its line of demarcation from other parts should be as marked as that which contemporary science draws between conscious and unconscious psychic activity. The animistic soul, on the contrary, unites determinants from both sides. Its flightiness and mobility, its faculty of leaving the body, of permanently or temporarily taking possession of another body, all these are characteristics which remind us unmistakably of the nature of consciousness. But the way in which it keeps itself concealed behind the personal appearance reminds us of the unconscious; today we no longer ascribe its unchangeableness and indestructibility

---

[36] "Principles of Sociology," Vol. I.

[37] Herbert Spencer, 1. c., p. 179.

[38] Compare my short paper: "A Note on the Unconscious in Psychoanalysis," in the Proceedings of the Society for Psychical Research, Part LXVI, Vol. XXVI, London, 1912.

to conscious but to unconscious processes and look upon these as the real bearers of psychic activity.

We said before that animism is a system of thought, the first complete theory of the world; we now want to draw certain inferences through psychoanalytic interpretation of such a system. Our everyday experience is capable of constantly showing us the main characteristics of the "system." We dream during the night and have learnt to interpret the dream in the daytime. The dream can, without being untrue to its nature, appear confused and incoherent; but on the other hand it can also imitate the order of impressions of an experience, infer one occurrence from another, and refer one part of its content to another. The dream succeeds more or less in this, but hardly ever succeeds so completely that an absurdity or a gap in the structure does not appear somewhere. If we subject the dream to interpretation we find that this unstable and irregular order of its components is quite unimportant for our understanding of it. The essential part of the dream are the dream thoughts, which have, to be sure, a significant, coherent order. But their order is quite different from that which we remember from the manifest content of the dream. The coherence of the dream thoughts has been abolished and may either remain altogether lost or can be replaced by the new coherence of the dream content. Besides the condensation of the dream elements there is almost regularly a re-grouping of the same which is more or less independent of the former order. We say in conclusion, that what the dream-work has made out of the material of the dream thoughts has been subjected to a new influence, the so-called "secondary elaboration," the object of which evidently is to do away with the incoherence and incomprehensibility caused by the dream- work, in favor of a new "meaning." This new meaning which has been brought about by the secondary elaboration is no longer the meaning of the dream thoughts.

The secondary elaboration of the product of the dream-work is an excellent example of the nature and the pretensions of a system. An intellectual function in us demands the unification, coherence and comprehensibility of everything perceived and thought of, and does not hesitate to construct a false connection if, as a result of special circumstances, it cannot grasp the right one. We know such system formations not only from the dream, but also from phobias, from compulsive thinking and from the types of delusions. The system formation is most ingenious in delusional states (paranoia) and dominates the clinical picture, but it also must not be overlooked in other forms of neuropsychoses. In every case we can show that a re- arrangement of the psychic material takes place, which may often be quite violent, provided it seems comprehensible from the point of view of the system. The best indication that a system has been formed then lies in the fact that each result of it can be shown to have at least two motivations one of which springs from the assumptions of the system and is therefore eventually delusional,—and a hidden one which, however, we must recognize as the real and effective motivation.

An example from a neurosis may serve as illustration. In the chapter on taboo I mentioned a patient whose compulsive prohibitions correspond very neatly to the taboo of the Maori.[39] The neurosis of this woman was directed against her husband and culminated in the defense against the unconscious wish for his death. But her manifest systematic phobia concerned the mention of death in general, in which her husband was altogether eliminated and never became the object of conscious solicitude. One day she heard her husband give an order to have his dull razors taken to a certain shop to have them sharpened. Impelled by a peculiar unrest she went to the shop herself and on her return from this

---

[39] p. 26.

reconnoiter she asked her husband to lay the razors aside for good because she had discovered that there was a warehouse of coffins and funeral accessories next to the shop he mentioned. She claimed that he had intentionally brought the razors into permanent relation with the idea of death. This was then the systematic motivation of the prohibition, but we may be sure that the patient would have brought home the prohibition relating to the razors even if she had not discovered this warehouse in the neighborhood. For it would have been sufficient if on her way to the shop she had met a hearse, a person in mourning, or somebody carrying a wreath. The net of determinants was spread out far enough to catch the prey in any case, it was simply a question whether she should pull it in or not. It could be established with certainty that she did not mobilize the determinants of the prohibition in other circumstances. She would then have said that it had been one of her "better days." The real reason for the prohibition of the razor was, of course, as we can easily guess, her resistance against a pleasurably accentuated idea that her husband might cut his throat with the sharpened razors.

In much the same way a motor inhibition, an abasia or an agoraphobia, becomes perfected and detailed if the symptom once succeeds in representing an unconscious wish and of imposing a defense against it. All the patient's remaining unconscious phantasies and effective reminiscences strive for symptomatic expression through this outlet, when once it has been opened, and range themselves appropriately in the new order within the sphere of the disturbance of gait. It would therefore be a futile and really foolish way to begin to try to understand the symptomatic structure and the details of, let us say, an agoraphobia, in terms of its basic assumptions. For the whole logic and strictness of connection is only apparent. Sharper observation can reveal, as in the formation of the facade in the dream, the greatest inconsistency and arbitrariness in the symptom formation. The details of such a systematic phobia take their real motivation from concealed determinants which must have nothing to do with the inhibition in gait; it is for this reason that the form of such a phobia varies so and is so contradictory in different people.

If we now attempt to retrace the system of animism with which we are concerned, we may conclude from our insight into other psychological systems that "superstition" need not be the only and actual motivation of such a single rule or custom even among primitive races, and that we are not relieved of the obligation of seeking for concealed motives. Under the dominance of an animistic system it is absolutely essential that each rule and activity should receive a systematic motivation which we to-day call "superstitious." But "superstition," like "anxiety," "dreams," and "demons," is one of the preliminaries of psychology which have been dissipated by psychoanalytic investigation. If we get behind these structures, which like a screen conceal understanding, we realize that the psychic life and the cultural level of savages have hitherto been inadequately appreciated.

If we regard the repression of impulses as a measure of the level of culture attained, we must admit that under the animistic system too, progress and evolution have taken place, which unjustly have been under-estimated on account of their superstitious motivation. If we hear that the warriors of a savage tribe impose the greatest chastity and cleanliness upon themselves as soon as they go upon the war-path,[40] the obvious explanation is that they dispose of their refuse in order that the enemy may not come into possession of this part of their person in order to harm them by magical means, and we may surmise analogous superstitious motivations for their abstinence. Nevertheless the fact remains that the impulse is

---

[40] Frazer, "Taboo and the Perils of the Soul," p. 158.

renounced and we probably understand the case better if we assume that the savage warrior imposes such restrictions upon himself in compensation, because he is on the point of allowing himself the full satisfaction of cruel and hostile impulses otherwise forbidden. The same holds good for the numerous cases of sexual restriction while he is pre-occupied with difficult or responsible tasks.[41] Even if the basis of these prohibitions can be referred to some association with magic, the fundamental conception of gaining greater strength by foregoing gratification of desires nevertheless remains unmistakable, and besides the magic rationalization of the prohibition, one must not neglect its hygienic root. When the men of a savage tribe go away to hunt, fish, make war or collect valuable plants, the women at home are in the meantime subjected to numerous oppressive restrictions which, according to the savages themselves, exert a sympathetic effect upon the success of the far away expedition. But it does not require much acumen to guess that this element acting at a distance is nothing but a thought of home, the longing of the absent, and that these disguises conceal the sound psychological insight that the men will do their best only if they are fully assured of the whereabouts of their guarded women. On other occasions the thought is directly expressed without magic motivation, that the conjugal infidelity of the wife thwarts the absent husband's efforts.

The countless taboo rules to which the women of savages are subject during their menstrual periods are motivated by the superstitious dread of blood which in all probability actually determines it. But it would be wrong to overlook the possibility that this blood dread also serves aesthetic and hygienic purposes which in every case have to be covered by magic motivations.

---

[41] Frazer, 1. c., p. 200.

We are probably not mistaken in assuming that such attempted explanations expose us to the reproach of attributing a most improbable delicacy of psychic activities to contemporary savages.

But I think that we may easily make the same mistake with the psychology of these races who have remained at the animistic stage that we made with the psychic life of the child, which we adults understood no better and whose richness and fineness of feeling we have therefore so greatly undervalued.

I want to consider another group of hitherto unexplained taboo rules because they admit of an explanation with which the psychoanalyst is familiar. Under certain conditions it is forbidden to many savage races to keep in the house sharp weapons and instruments for cutting.[42] Frazer cites a German superstition that a knife must not be left lying with the edge pointing upward because God and the angels might injure themselves with it. May we not recognize in this taboo a premonition of certain "symptomatic actions"[43] for which the sharp weapon might be used by unconscious evil impulses?

---

[42] Frazer, 1. c., p. 237.

[43] Freud, "Psychopathology of Everyday Life," p. 215, trans, by A. A. Brill (The Macmillan Company, N. Y., and T. Fisher Unwin, London).

www.ingramcontent.com/pod-product-compliance
Lightning Source LLC
LaVergne TN
LVHW041503070426
835507LV00009B/775